DATE DUE		
FEB 2 7	APR 4 '01	
APR 2 4 '9	MAY 09	
SEP 4	AUG 0 9 2001	
SEP 4 '97		
APR 9 9		
FEB 2 '9		
JUL 06 '99		
AUG 12		
AUG 3 0 '99		
NOV 23		

8/96

Jackson

County

Library

System

HEADQUARTERS:

413 W. Main

Medford, Oregon 97501

GAYLORD M2G

Geology

Graham Peacock and Jill Jesson

Thomson Learning • New York

Books in the series:

ASTRONOMY • ELECTRICITY • FORCES
GEOLOGY • HEAT • LIGHT • MATERIALS
METEOROLOGY • SOUND • WATER

First published in the
United States in 1995 by
Thomson Learning
115 Fifth Avenue
New York, NY 10003

First published in Great Britain in 1994 by
Wayland (Publishers) Ltd.

Library of Congress Cataloging-in-Publication Data
Peacock, Graham.
  Geology / Graham Peacock and Jill Jesson.
    p.   cm. – (Science activities)
  Includes bibliographical references and index.
  ISBN: 1-56847-193-9
  1. Geology – Juvenile literature. 2. Geology –
Experiments. [1. Geology – Experiments.
2. Experiments] I. Jesson, Jill. II. Title. III. Series.
QE29.P424   1995
550 – dc20   94-30608

Printed in Italy

Acknowledgments
The publishers would like to thank the following for allowing their pictures to be used in this book: Geoscience Features Ltd. *cover*; Tony Stone Worldwide p. 18; Zefa *cover* (top), p. 15, p. 20, p. 24. All commissioned photographs are from the Wayland Picture Library (Zul Mukhida). All artwork is by Tony de Saulles.

Contents

Words that appear in **bold** are explained in the glossary
on page 30.

Long ago

Geology is the study of the earth. It includes the study of forces of the earth, such as **volcanoes** and **earthquakes**, which are so huge they can destroy cities. The study of **rocks** gives clues about the way the rocks were formed. **Fossils** of long-dead animals and plants can tell you about the way life began billions of years ago and how it has been changing ever since.

How old is the earth?

You will need:

◆ a large sheet of cardboard ◆ 184 in. of string
◆ colored felt-tip pens ◆ tape ◆ a ruler

1 With one end of the string representing 4.6 billion years ago and using a scale of 1 inch = 25 billion years, mark off seven measurements as shown at right.

2 Use felt-tipped pens to color the seven sections of string different colors.

3 Tape the string to cardboard as shown.

4 Write in the Earth Events Highlights beside the string, as in the diagram.

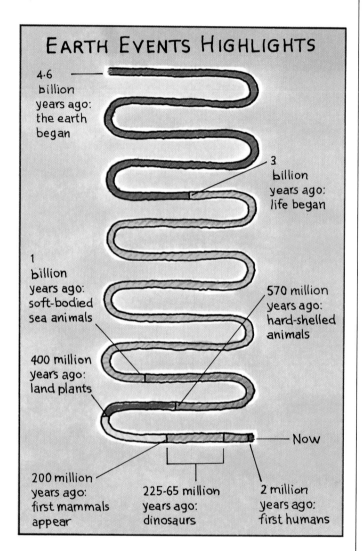

EARTH EVENTS HIGHLIGHTS

4.6 billion years ago: the earth began

3 billion years ago: life began

1 billion years ago: soft-bodied sea animals

570 million years ago: hard-shelled animals

400 million years ago: land plants

Now

200 million years ago: first mammals appear

225-65 million years ago: dinosaurs

2 million years ago: first humans

Did you know?

If you made a string chart where 1 inch = 1 year, you would need nearly 73,000 miles of string. That would be enough to go around the equator almost three times.

How is geological time divided?

Era	Period	Millions of years ago
Cenozoic	Tertiary	Now Huge volcanoes. Mammals develop into many types. 65
Mesozoic	Cretaceous	First flowering plants develop. Ammonites swimming in clear seas. Dinosaurs disappear at end of period. 135
Mesozoic	Jurassic	Dinosaurs rule the land. First birds develop. 195
Mesozoic	Triassic	Dinosaurs and mammals develop. Reptiles spread. 225
Paleozoic	Permian	280
Paleozoic	Carboniferous	Dark swamps of tall trees and ferns. Amphibians spread. First insects. 345
Paleozoic	Devonian	Trees and low green plants on land. Fish in sea. Amphibians appear. 395
Paleozoic	Silurian	First land plants. First fish. 435
Paleozoic	Ordovician	Trilobites, shellfish, and other invertebrates in sea. 500
Paleozoic	Cambrian	Algae and invertebrate animals in sea. 570
	Pre-Cambrian	

You will need:

◆ a sheet of paper ◆ a ruler ◆ a pen

1 This chart shows what it was like in parts of Europe and North America at different times in the earth's history.

2 Make a series of larger pictures showing what it was like in each period.

Make a time chart of the twentieth century, like the one below, and put your family's history on it.

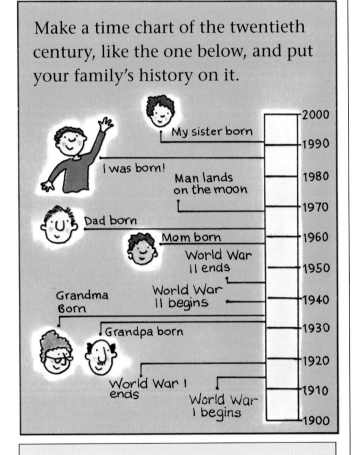

Death from the sky

Many **geologists** believe that on at least two occasions huge **meteorites** struck the earth. These caused many plants and animals including dinosaurs to become extinct.

5

Being a geologist

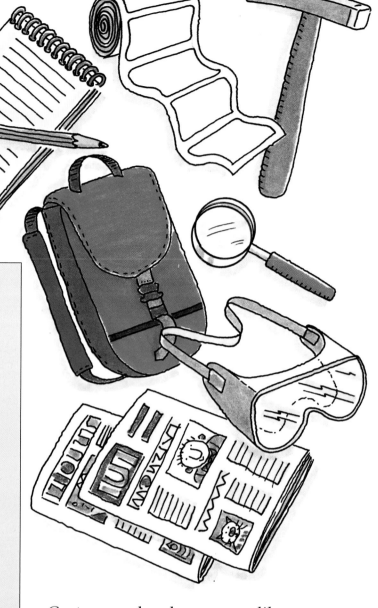

What do you need?

- a notebook and pencil
- labels
- newspapers
- a strong bag
- a magnifying glass
- a geological hammer
- goggles to protect your eyes

Golden rules for rockhounds

1 Ask an adult to accompany you.

2 Get permission to visit quarries or sites on private land.

3 Be careful on cliffs and watch out for the tide on beaches.

4 Try not to hammer rock faces – many samples can be found on the ground.

5 Only hammer samples on the ground, not on a rock face.

6 Protect your eyes with goggles.

Go to your local museum, library, or tourist information center to discover which rocks are in your area.

When collecting

Wrap each sample in newspaper, and add a label stating where you found it.

At home

Wash specimens gently in soapy water with a nailbrush or an old toothbrush.

Make a museum

You will need:

◆ specimens of rocks and crystals ◆ a clear plastic container ◆ an old drawer ◆ labels ◆ a wide glass jar or tumbler filled with water ◆ a notebook ◆ a pencil

1 Put your largest specimens in the clear plastic container.

2 Set out specimens in the drawer.

3 Put any beach pebbles in the jar of water to show their colors best.

4 Label each specimen, stating where and when you found it.

5 Keep a geological notebook to record information about your specimens. Use one page for each specimen.

World map

You will need:

◆ rock specimens from different countries (you can get these from a geological supplier) ◆ a world atlas ◆ tracing paper ◆ a pencil ◆ colored thread ◆ labels ◆ cardboard

1 Trace a world map from the atlas.

2 Use the thread and labels to show where each specimen came from, as in the diagram below.

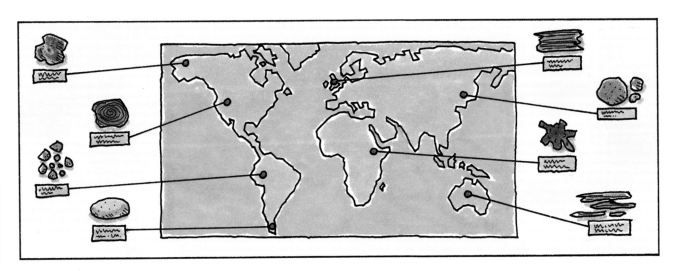

Minerals and crystals

What are minerals?

Minerals are chemical compounds that form crystals. Pyrite is a mineral that is a compound of iron and sulfur.

Pyrite forms shiny, brassy crystals in the shape of cubes and is sometimes called fool's gold.

Pan for minerals

You will need:

◆ a basin ◆ a shallow bowl ◆ a bag of lentils or rice ◆ a pitcher of water
◆ a small quantity of sand and gravel ◆ some small pieces of metal, such as screws, nuts, or nails

1 Mix together the lentils, sand, gravel, and metal pieces in the bowl.

2 Hold this bowl over the basin and have someone pour water slowly into the bowl.

3 Keep pouring the water until all the light material has washed out into the basin. What is left in the bowl?

Gold prospectors

Panning is still used to find gold pieces. Gold is very heavy so it is unlikely to be washed out of the pan.

Gold is very rare. It makes up only 0.000005% of the earth's surface.

What shapes do crystals form?

Crystals are elements or **compounds** that have a regular shape and flat faces. **Salt** and sugar are crystals we use every day. Common table salt is a crystal compound made from the elements sodium and chlorine.

The shape of a crystal depends on the way its atoms are arranged. Salt's atoms are arranged like this:

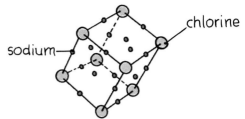

Grow a big crystal

You will need:

◆ alum (from a pharmacy) ◆ a measuring cup ◆ a glass jar ◆ a wide, shallow dish ◆ a spoon ◆ a notebook and pencil ◆ string ◆ water

1 Stir as much **alum** as will dissolve into about 2 tablespoons of water.

2 Pour the solution into the dish and let it evaporate for two days.

3 Select the best crystal left in the dish and let it dry.

4 Tie a piece of string to the crystal and hang it in the jar with a solution of alum and water for a week.

5 Draw the shape of the crystal.

Did you know?

Diamonds are the hardest known material in the world. They are a crystalline form of carbon. Diamonds are so hard that they are used in industrial cutting machines.

Rocks

Rocks are made from minerals. They can be formed in three ways:

Igneous rocks	**Sedimentary rocks**	**Metamorphic rocks**

- Formed from molten material (magma or lava)
- Made from crystals that have grown together.
- Often hard.
- Never contain fossils.
- Not usually layered.

- Formed when other rocks are worn away and their remains are deposited as sediments.
- Grains can be rubbed off.
- Often have clear layers.
- Often contain fossils.

- Formed from igneous and sedimentary rocks that have been changed in some way by heat or pressure.
- Often streaked or banded.
- Usually hard.

Ignis is the Latin word for fire.

Sedo is Latin for settle down.

Meta is Greek for change. *Morphe* means form.

Testing rocks

You will need:

- a collection of rocks (not valuable specimens) ◆ a coin
- a steel nail or blunt knife ◆ a magnifying glass
- a dropper ◆ soapy water ◆ a nailbrush
- a bowl of clear vinegar

Hardness

1 Which of your rocks can you scratch with your fingernail? These are very soft rocks.

2 Which can be scratched with the coin? These are soft rocks.

3 Which can be scratched only with the nail or knife? These are hard rocks.

Do your rocks fizz in vinegar?

1 Clean your rocks in soapy water with the nailbrush.

2 Carefully place them in the bowl of vinegar. Do any of them fizz?

Limestone is made of the mineral calcium carbonate. This is dissolved by acids such as vinegar. Chalk is a form of limestone.

Do your rocks soak up water?

1 Use the dropper to put a big drop of water on each rock sample.

2 Look at each drop half an hour later. Which has soaked up the water? Which did not?

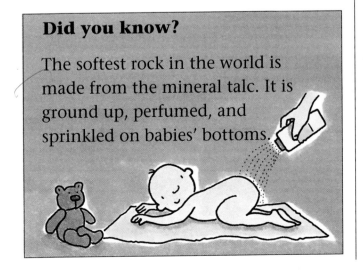

Did you know?

The softest rock in the world is made from the mineral talc. It is ground up, perfumed, and sprinkled on babies' bottoms.

Some rocks absorb water. These rocks are a natural underground store of water.

Igneous and metamorphic rocks

What is granite made of?

You will need:

◆ a collection of igneous rocks, including granite and pumice ◆ a bowl of water ◆ a magnifying glass ◆ a steel nail

Granite is a type of igneous rock. It is made from three main crystals:

• quartz
• feldspar
• mica

1 Look at the sample of granite above.

2 Look at the two minerals, quartz and feldspar, below.

Can you see the quartz and feldspar in the granite?

Investigate pumice

1 How heavy is **pumice** compared with other rocks?

2 Does it float in water? Try it and see.

3 How hard is it? Test it with the nail.

You can buy pumice at a pharmacy. It is used to rub off dead skin. Pumice is a **volcanic rock** that cooled from lava full of gas bubbles.

Origin of igneous rock

Magma rises

Ash and thick lava form steep cones.

Runny lava flows. Some form hexagonal columns like the Giant's Causeway in Ireland.

Granite forms deep underground as magma and is trapped under rock.

12

What is slate?

You will need:

◆ a collection of metamorphic rocks, including marble and slate ◆ a blunt steel knife

1 Carefully scrape the **slate** with the knife. Feel how fine the dust is.

2 Look for evidence that slate began as a sedimentary rock. Are there any layers of different colors?

Slate is a metamorphic rock. It is mudstone that has been pressed and heated.

Slate tiles are used for roofing because slate is waterproof and splits into thin sheets, so it is easy to build with. Is there any slate near your home or school?

Why does slate split?

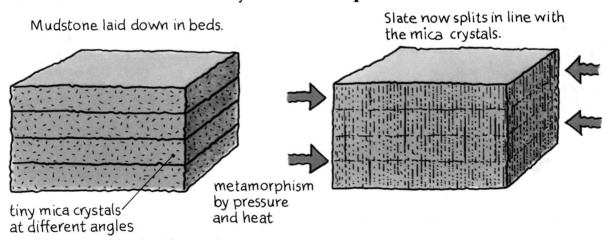

Mudstone laid down in beds.

tiny mica crystals at different angles

metamorphism by pressure and heat

Slate now splits in line with the mica crystals.

What is marble?

Marble is a metamorphic limestone.

1 Look for the crystals in the marble (it is easier to see them in a broken piece).

2 How hard is it? Test it with the knife.

Pure limestone forms white marble. Impurities in the limestone form streaked marble. It is used for buildings, statues, and tabletops all over the world.

Sedimentary rocks

Rock sort

You will need:

◆ a collection of sedimentary rocks, including mudstone, shale, and sandstone

Sort your sedimentary rocks into groups according to the size of their grains:

- Mudstone is a fine-grained sedimentary rock.

- Shale is a fine-grained rock with flaky layers.

- Sandstone is made of sand pressed together. It has larger grains than mudstone or shale. Sandstone's crystals glimmer in bright lights.

How are ripple marks formed?

You will need:

◆ 3 tablespoons clean sand ◆ a large circular bowl
◆ a pitcher of water ◆ a large spoon

1 Stand the jug of water in the bowl.

2 Fill the bowl halfway with water.

3 Sprinkle the sand into the bowl.

4 Stir the sand and water in one direction around the bowl.

5 Take out the spoon and watch what happens to the sand.

6 Draw the shape of the ripples.

Can you figure out the direction of the water flow from looking at these ripples?

Ripple marks in sedimentary rocks show the direction in which the water was flowing when the sediment was first deposited.

What causes stalactites and stalagmites?

You will need:
- Epsom salts ◆ a spoon
- 2 glasses filled with warm water
- a plate ◆ thick string, 20 inches long
- thin string, 20 inches long

1 Dissolve as much Epsom salts as you can into the two glasses of warm water.

2 Hang the thick string between the two glasses, making sure the ends are in both solutions.

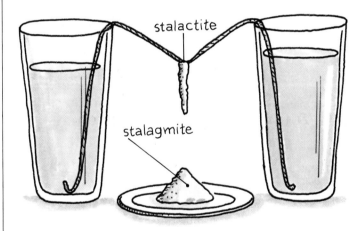

3 Place the plate under the lowest part of the string. Wait several days.

4 What do you think will happen if you use the thinner string? Try coloring the solution with food dye.

Stalactites and **stalagmites** are formed when water containing dissolved limestone drips from a cave roof. Some of the water evaporates, leaving behind a tiny layer of limestone. Stalagmites build upward from cave floors. Stalactites hang from cave ceilings.

These stalactites and stalagmites have taken thousands of years to form.

How long does sedimentary rock take to form?

Chalk is a white sedimentary rock that formed about 100 million years ago in many places throughout the world.

Chalk is the slow buildup of the skeletons of tiny sea creatures. About half an inch depth of chalk has formed every 1,000 years.

15

Fossils

Fossils are the remains left by long-dead plants or animals. They may be actual remains, such as bones or teeth, or marks, such as footprints or shell prints.

Make a fossil

You will need:

◆ clay ◆ a shell or a leaf ◆ plaster of paris
◆ a disposable cup ◆ a disposable spoon

1 Squash the clay into a slab that is bigger than the shell.

2 Build the walls of the slab up higher than the middle.

3 Carefully press the shell into the middle of the slab. Remove it.

4 Mix the plaster of paris with water in the cup.

5 Pour it into the mold. Allow it to set for an hour.

6 Carefully remove the fossil.

Did you know?

The fossil "Lucy" was found in Ethiopia in 1974. Lucy was an adult who lived 3 million years ago. She was 3-4 feet tall and nearly human, but she had some apelike features.

Keep a record of your fossils in a notebook. Store your fossils in labeled compartments.

What do fossils tell you?

Fossils can give you clues about what was living and what the world was like when rocks were laid down. All these fossils were once sea creatures.

Trilobites are now extinct and can only be found in rocks that are 225–570 million years old. Their closest relative is the king crab.

Ammonites became extinct 65 million years ago. They were like squid with shells.

Corals still exist today. Rocks that contain coral fossils were laid down in warm, clear, and clean seas.

Bony fish only became common about 400 million years ago.

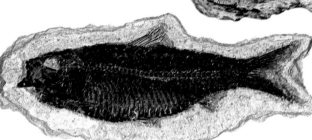

Dinosaur fossils

You will need:

◈ a measuring tape

1 Look at the dinosaurs in the table.

2 Find out which dinosaurs would fit in your
• bedroom • cafeteria • school playground

Dinosaur	Length
Micropachycephalosaurus	1.5 feet
Triceratops	30 feet
Diplodocus	90 feet

Brachiosaur

Tyrannosaurus, up to 20 feet tall

Composgnathus, 2 feet from nose to tail

50 feet

85 feet

Folds and faults

Folds

Most sedimentary and volcanic rocks were laid down flat. Movements in the earth's crust cause them to bend and buckle.

You will need:

◆ clay in 3 different colors

1 Make a block of three layers of clay.

2 Bend it to make a fold. Where does the clay crack? This is how some mountains are formed.

Making mountains

You will need:

◆ a piece of thick cloth

When two continents collide, the rocks between them are crumpled up into mountain ranges. Push the cloth together from the sides to make a mountain range with the folds.

Did you know?

Fossils of sea creatures can be found high up in many mountain ranges. The rock in which they were formed was laid down under the sea.

The Himalayas were formed when massive earth movements pushed up huge folds of rock.

Faults

Faults are cracks in the rocks of the earth's crust where the rocks slip past each other.

You will need:
- clay in 3 different colors
- a blunt knife

1 Make a block of three layers.

2 Cut it into three parts. Move the middle section down.

3 This is how a rift valley is formed: two blocks of earth rise up while the middle block sinks.

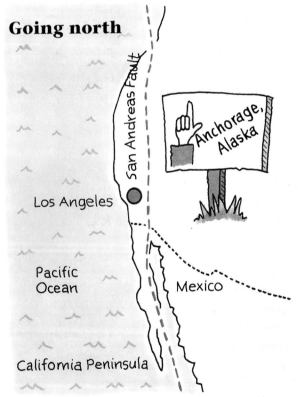

Going north

Los Angeles and the California Peninsula are moving past the rest of California at about 2 inches each year. At this rate Los Angeles will be near Anchorage, Alaska, in about 60 million years.

Moving continents

You will need:
- a world atlas ◆ 2 pieces of tracing paper
- a pencil ◆ scissors

1 Trace the outlines of Africa and South America onto separate pieces of tracing paper. Make sure you trace maps that have the same scale. Cut them out.

2 Try to fit the two continents together like a jigsaw puzzle.

Most geologists think that South America and Africa were once joined in a super continent.

19

Earthquakes and volcanoes

Volcano map

You will need:
- tracing paper
- a pencil
- a world atlas

1 Trace the map of the Pacific region on the right.

2 Look in the index of the atlas to find the volcanoes listed below:
Mount Fuji (Japan),
Katmai (Alaska),
Mount St. Helens (Washington State),
Paricutin (Mexico), Villanca (Chile).

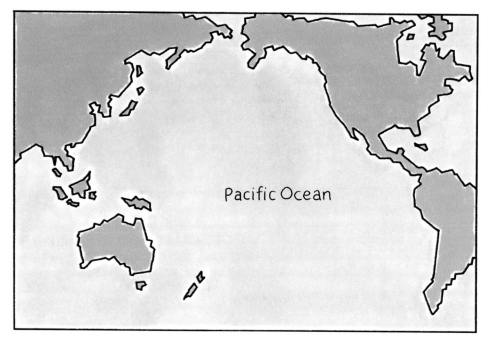

Pacific Ocean

3 Mark these volcanoes on your map using a symbol like the one on the right.

This area around the Pacific Ocean is called the Ring of Fire because volcanoes are most common there. This area also has the most earthquakes.

The molten lava that pours out of volcanoes has a temperature of over 3,600 °F.

Did you know?

The largest recent eruption occured in 1883 when the volcano Krakatoa exploded in Java and killed 35,000 people when tidal waves swept over nearby islands. The dust that was hurled into the atmosphere made the world's climate cooler for ten years afterward.

What causes earthquakes?

You will need:

◆ 3 bars of caramel ◆ a refrigerator and a freezer

1 Put one bar of caramel in the refrigerator, one in the freezer, and leave the other one out.

2 After an hour, try to bend each bar.

Which bar is most difficult to bend?

Do any of them snap?

Earthquakes happen when cold, stiff rocks in the earth's plates do not bend easily and shudder over one another.

Make a quake

You will need:

◆ 2 bricks ◆ a short, thick pen

1 Place one brick on top of the other. Stand the pen on the top brick.

2 Gently push the top brick so it slides over the bottom brick.

3 Notice how much it shudders and sticks. What happens to the pen?

The bricks are like the rocks on either side of a fault line. In an earthquake, the shuddering of the rocks causes buildings to fall over.

Soils and sands

What is soil? Are all soils the same?

You will need:

◈ soil and sand samples from several places, such as a flower bed, under a tree, by a stream
◈ a magnifying glass ◈ labels ◈ a pencil
◈ 1 tall or a few small glass jars ◈ a notebook
◈ a bowl of water ◈ a sheet of white paper

1 Look at each **soil** sample with the magnifying glass. Is there anything alive in the soil?

2 What shape and color are the grains?

3 What does each smell like?

4 Rub some between your fingers. How does each sample feel?

5 Roll each sample into a ball with a little water. Which soil makes the best ball?

6 Smear some of each soil on the piece of paper. Each may have a different color. This is known as its **streak**.

7 Put your samples in the tall jar in layers or in a few small jars. Label each sample with its name and the results of your tests.

Soil is composed of

• weathered rock

• air and water

• the remains of plants and animals

• tiny living creatures.

Drain test

You will need:

◆ 2 funnels (or cut off 2 plastic bottle tops) ◆ 2 glass jars ◆ 2 different soils (the test works best with a clay soil and a sandy soil) ◆ water ◆ 4 flower pots ◆ grass seeds

1 Put each soil in a different funnel, putting the same amount in each.

2 Rest the funnels in the jars and pour water through each soil. Discard the water.

3 Now pour the same amount of fresh water onto both soils at the same time. Which soil lets the water through faster? Do they both let the same amount through?

4 Which soil would be best for growing plants? Test your prediction by sowing the grass seeds in a variety of different soils.

What's in your soil?

You will need:

◆ 3 tablespoons of soil samples from several places, such as a flowerbed, under a tree, beside a stream ◆ a large glass jar ◆ a spoon ◆ a watch ◆ a notebook and pencil ◆ water

1 Put one soil sample into the jar.

2 Fill the jar with water, stir it, and let it settle.

3 Watch the order in which the materials settle.

4 How long does it take for the water to clear?

5 Is there anything floating on the top?

6 Test the other soil samples in the same way. Make notes and diagrams to compare your results.

Geology in towns

Be a geological detective

You will need:

◆ a notebook and pencil
◆ an adult to accompany you

1 Look at the buildings in your area.

We are surrounded by rocks, even in cities, towns, and villages.

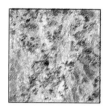 Granite: coarse, interlocking crystals.

 Slate: thin sheets of dark rock.

 Tiles: made from thin sheets of clay.

 Limestone: smooth, cream or gray.

 Concrete: made from lime, sand, and water.

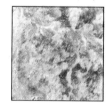 Asphalt: covering of pebbles and cement.

 Sandstone: layers of sand pressed together.

 Brick: made from clay; can be red or yellow.

 Marble: smooth, with veins and patterns.

2 Make a list of stones and make a check next to each one you find.

3 What is each stone used for?

4 What differences can you see between those which are natural and those which are manufactured?

The Taj Mahal, in India, is built of white marble, a metamorphic form of limestone. It was built by an emperor of India as a tomb for his adored wife. It took 20,000 people more than 15 years to build.

Erosion

5 Which parts of the buildings are wearing away? Look for clues in the stones and what is causing a change in them.

6 Look at doorways, steps, paths, and roofs. What do you think is causing **erosion**?

Erosion is caused by rain, wind, tree roots, people walking, and acid rain.

Ornamental rocks

You will need:
◈ a notebook and pencil

1 Visit a cemetery and look at the headstones.

2 Take a survey of the stones you see used.

How have fashions changed over the years?

3 What types of stone were popular:

• 50 years ago?
• 100 years ago?
• 150 years ago?

4 Which types of stone show signs of erosion? Are they the oldest?

Rocks erode at different rates.

Date	Type of Stone	Erosion?
1850	sandstone	X X X X
1900	marble	X
1940	limestone	X X
1955	slate	X

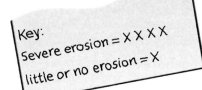

Key:
Severe erosion = X X X X
little or no erosion = X

Rock invaders

Plants like to grow on stone. First algae, then lichen, moss, and larger plants like ivy will invade bare rock. In time, this will break the rock down to form new soil.

Which invaders can you find on the headstones? Draw them.

Geology in the countryside

Make a changing landscape

You will need:

◆ a large plastic basin ◆ a large rock
◆ earth, clay, and sand ◆ a watering can

1 Place the rock on the basin and cover it with layers of earth, clay, and sand.

2 Give your landscape a shower of rain from the watering can.

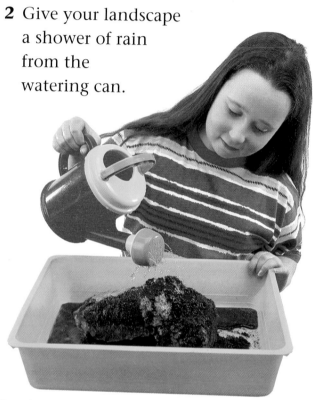

See how:

• The surface soil is washed away and deposited farther down.
• The rock underneath is exposed.
• A river system is created that drains through channels to a "sea" below.
• Debris builds up in a delta in the sea.

Landscapes are constantly changing. Weathering helps to break down old landscapes. Erosion moves the particles to form new landscapes.

Rock shattering: which is the strongest rock?

You will need:

◆ several types of rocks, such as sandstone, limestone, chalk, granite, and slate
◆ an old pan with lid, filled with pebbles

1 Put three or four pieces of one type of rock in the pan.

2 Put the lid on and shake the pan twenty times.

3 Now do it for each rock type in turn.

4 Look at each rock type. Which has worn away the most?

Which rocks would form hills and headlands in a landscape? Which rocks would form bays and valleys?

On the beach

You will need:

◆ a sandy beach ◆ a spade

Dig near the sea and far from it. How deep do you have to dig before you reach water in each case? What do you notice?

Rain sinks under the ground to the water table. This can be deep down. On a beach it is near the surface.

You will need:

◆ a pebble beach

Make a collection of pebbles. Are pebbles of the same shape formed from the same type of rock? On a pebble beach, you may find stones that have been brought by the sea from many miles away.

Did you know?

Shellfish called piddocks bore into rock. The hole they make at first is smaller than their eventual size, so they are locked into the rock forever.

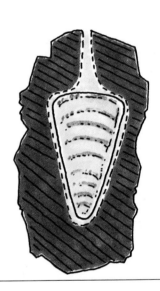

True or False?

1 A trilobite is a fish you can buy in the supermarket.
2 The earth is about 4.6 billion years old.
3 Granite is an igneous rock.
4 Limestone dissolves in vinegar.
5 Granite has a coarse texture.
6 Shale is a volcanic rock.
7 The fossil "Lucy" is ten years old.
8 The Taj Mahal is made of a metamorphic rock.

The answers are on page 32.

Naming rocks and fossils

Rocks

You will need:

◆ a collection of various rocks and fossils

◆ a notebook and pencil

Use this key to identify each rock and fossil in your collection:

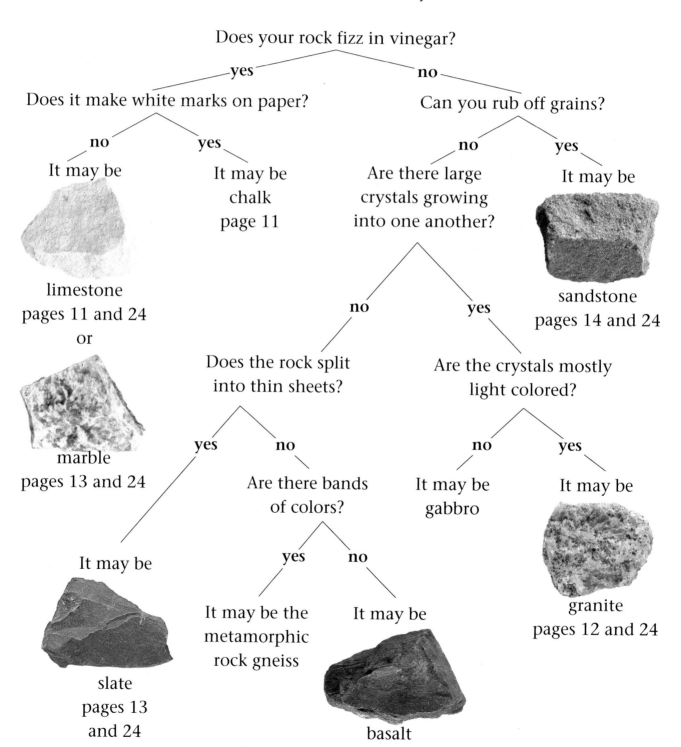

Does your rock fizz in vinegar?

yes — no

Does it make white marks on paper?

no — yes

It may be

limestone
pages 11 and 24
or

marble
pages 13 and 24

It may be
chalk
page 11

Can you rub off grains?

no — yes

Are there large
crystals growing
into one another?

It may be

sandstone
pages 14 and 24

no — yes

Does the rock split
into thin sheets?

Are the crystals mostly
light colored?

yes — no

It may be

slate
pages 13
and 24

Are there bands
of colors?

yes — no

It may be the
metamorphic
rock gneiss

It may be

basalt

no — yes

It may be
gabbro

It may be

granite
pages 12 and 24

Fossils

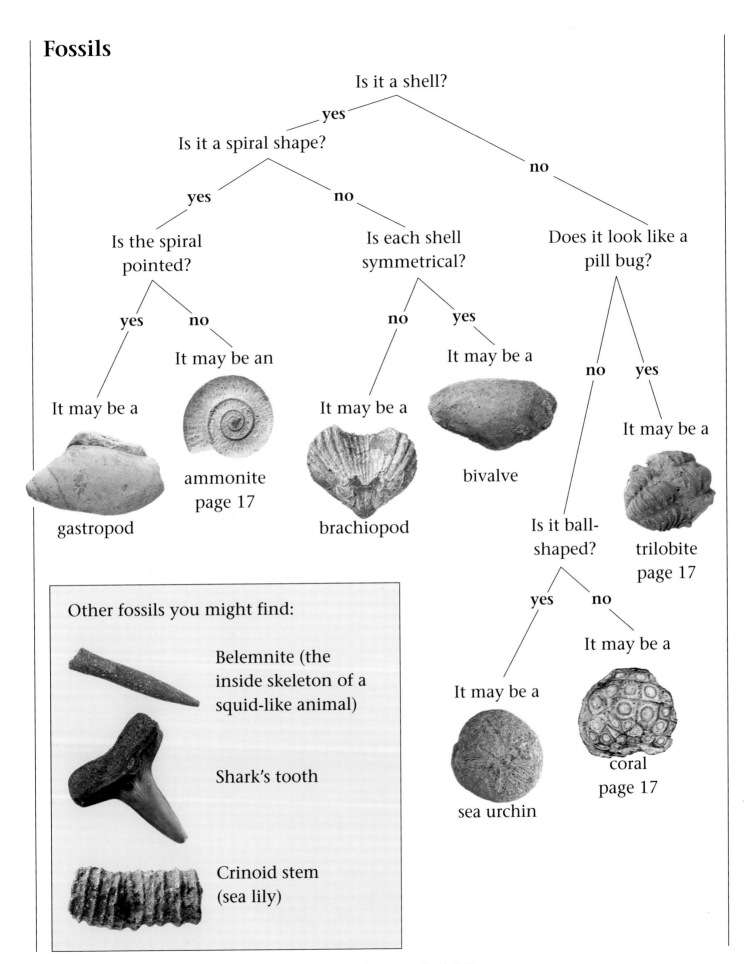

Is it a shell?

yes → Is it a spiral shape?

no → Does it look like a pill bug?

Is it a spiral shape?
- **yes** → Is the spiral pointed?
- **no** → Is each shell symmetrical?

Is the spiral pointed?
- **yes** → It may be a gastropod
- **no** → It may be an ammonite page 17

Is each shell symmetrical?
- **no** → It may be a brachiopod
- **yes** → It may be a bivalve

Does it look like a pill bug?
- **no** → Is it ball-shaped?
- **yes** → It may be a trilobite page 17

Is it ball-shaped?
- **yes** → It may be a sea urchin
- **no** → It may be a coral page 17

Other fossils you might find:

Belemnite (the inside skeleton of a squid-like animal)

Shark's tooth

Crinoid stem (sea lily)

Glossary

Alum Potassium aluminum silicate. It forms large, eight-sided crystals.

Ammonites Extinct cephalopods similar to the present-day nautilus.

Compounds Substances made from the combination of two or more elements.

Crystals A mineral that has a definite regular shape.

Earthquakes Sudden violent movements of the earth's crust caused when two large masses of rock slide past each other.

Erosion The movement of weathered rock.

Fossils The remains or the traces of the remains of animals or plants.

Geologists People who study the earth.

Granite A coarse-grained igneous rock that cooled from magma deep in the earth's crust.

Lava Molten rock that has erupted on to the earth's surface.

Limestone A sedimentary rock formed largely from the mineral calcium carbonate. This mineral fizzes in acid.

Magma Molten rock that stays beneath the surface of the earth.

Meteorites Pieces of rock that fall from space onto the surface of the earth.

Minerals Naturally occurring chemical compounds (e.g., salt) or elements (e.g., gold).

Pumice A very light, volcanic rock formed from a very frothy lava.

Rocks A collection of minerals.

Salt Common table salt is sodium chloride, a compound made from atoms of the elements sodium and chlorine.

Slate A hard metamorphic rock that has been formed from mudstone. It splits along lines.

Soil A mixture of ground-down rock fragments and plant remains.

Stalactites Limestone pillars that hang from cave ceilings.

Stalagmites Limestone pillars that build up from cave floors.

Streak The color left on paper when a mineral or soil is rubbed across it.

Trilobites Extinct animals that lived in the sea. They were arthropods similar to horseshoe crabs today.

Volcanic rock An igneous rock formed from lava.

Volcanoes An opening in the earth's surface from which molten material from deep inside the earth erupts as lava to spread to the surface, sometimes forming a cone or mountain.

Books to read

Catherall, Ed. *Exploring Soil and Rocks*. Exploring Science. Raintree Steck-Vaughn, 1990.

Dudman, John. *Volcano*. Violent Earth. New York: Thomson Learning, 1993.

Farndon, John. *How the Earth Works: One Hundred Ways Parents and Kids Can Share the Secrets of the Earth*. New York: Reader's Digest Association, 1992.

Lauber, Pat. *Dinosaurs Walked Here and Other Stories Fossils Tell*. New York: Macmillan Publishing, 1992.

Lye, Keith. *The Earth*. Young Readers' Nature Library. Brookfield, CT: Millbrook Press, 1991.

Mariner, Tom. *Continents*. Earth in Action. North Bellmore, NY: Marshall Cavendish, 1990.

Newton, David E. *Earthquakes*. First Books. Franklin Watts, 1993.

Snedden, Robert. *The Super Science Book of the Rocks and Soils*. Super Science. Thomson Learning, 1994.

Chapter notes

Pages 4–5 Rocks and fossils give us good clues about what the surface of the earth was like in the geological past. It is likely that life existed on earth before 3 billion years ago, but this is the age of the earliest fossils. The first living things were single-cell bacteria and algae. There are several theories to explain the sudden large-scale extinctions that occurred at the end of the Permian and then again at the end of the Cretaceous periods.

Pages 6–7 Where possible, pick up fallen specimens. Never hammer without proper protective gear and permission from the landowner. Fossils are often very difficult to extract in one piece and it is usually better to leave them in the rock for others to see. Take care when cleaning and washing rocks that they do not dissolve in water.

Pages 8–9 Panning requires skill and patience. If possible, use some pieces of lead ore from a geological supplier. These are not as heavy as gold but will be better than screws and nuts. DO NOT DRINK THE ALUM SOLUTION.

Pages 10–11 Think of other ways to test rocks.

Pages 12–13 The mineralogy of igneous rocks is hugely variable. To complicate matters, rocks such as granite and obsidian (volcanic glass), which look quite dissimilar, share the same mineral composition. Basalt forms columnar jointing where a very liquid flow has cooled from the surface down. The rock contracts as it cools and tends to form circles. Equal-size circles will touch six others, resulting in six-sided joints.

Pages 14–15 The classic test to tell the difference between a sandstone and a mudstone is to rub a little of the rock with a drop of water. If it feels gritty between the fingers it is sandstone; if it becomes a paste it is mudstone. Fossil ripple marks in rocks are very useful to geologists who want to tell the direction of current flow.

Pages 16–17 Dinosaurs were extinct 63 million years before the first Stone Age people. Fossils that were free swimming, like ammonites, are very useful to match the dates of rocks in several different places. It is even better if the animals were evolving rapidly and changing their form, as was the case with ammonites. All ammonites died out in the great extinction at the end of the Cretaceous Period, along with the dinosaurs.

Pages 18–19 Faults can range in size from a small crack a few feet long to a massive dislocation between land masses. Many pieces of evidence suggest that the continents move across the earth's surface.

Pages 20–21 There is a clear relationship between the places where volcanoes are found and the areas in which earthquakes occur. The Pacific Ocean is closing up, resulting in the ocean floor being pushed under Asia. This causes the earthquakes and volcanoes of Southeast Asia. Scientists are still trying to predict earthquakes, but with relatively little success. It is not a question of whether, but when, there will be further earthquakes in California or Japan.

Pages 22–23 Try making your own soil from a mixture of soil or ground bricks and peat or rotted compost. A plug of cotton will help to keep the soil from falling out of the funnels in the drainage test.

Pages 24–25 Banks are one of the best places to find highly polished rocks. You will probably be surprised at the variety of rocks to be found decorating cities. Two hundred years ago, gravestones were almost all made from local stone. However this usually wore away quickly. In recent years, granite monuments have been used. These wear very slowly, even after several centuries of exposure.

Pages 26–27 If you want to carve chalk, it helps to soak it overnight in water or in a mixture of white paste and water. This cuts down the dust and makes it softer. You might want to use a chisel to make interesting effects.

Pages 28–29 These are simple branching keys that are used for many purposes of classification in science. Try to come up with your own branching key. Sort your collection in a variety of ways.

Index

Answers to questions on page 27:
1 False, **2** True, **3** True, **4** True, **5** True, **6** False, **7** False, **8** True